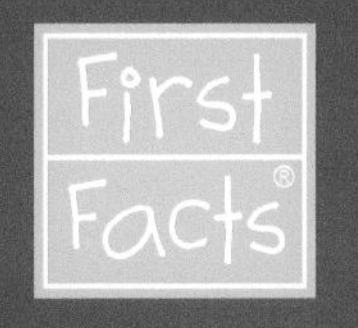

Staying Safe

Staying Safe on the Playground

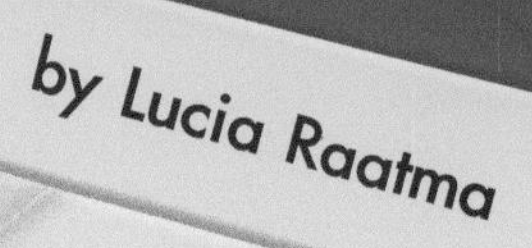

by Lucia Raatma

CAPSTONE PRESS
a capstone imprint

First Facts is published by Capstone Press,
1710 Roe Crest Drive, North Mankato, Minnesota 56003.
www.capstonepub.com

Library of Congress Cataloging-in-Publication Data
Raatma, Lucia.
Staying safe on the playground / by Lucia Raatma.
p. cm. — (First facts. staying safe)
Includes bibliographical references and index.
Summary: "Discusses rules and techniques for playground safety"—Provided by publisher.
ISBN 978-1-4296-6822-4 (library binding)
ISBN 978-1-4296-7197-2 (paperback)
1. Playgrounds—Safety measures—Juvenile literature. I. Title.
GV424.R24 2012
796.068—dc22 2011006045

Editorial Credits
Rebecca Glaser and Christine Peterson, editors; Ted Williams, designer;
Svetlana Zhurkin, media researcher; Laura Manthe, production specialist

Photo Credits
Capstone Studio/Karon Dubke, 1, 9, 18; Dreamstime/Countrymama, 15; Ferguswang, 6; Greenland, 14iStockphoto/Brian Butler, 16–17; Midhat Becar, 5; Vicki Reid, 8
Shutterstock/Juriah Mosin, cover; Monkey Business Images, 20; Neil Webster, 12; vblinov, 10–11

Essential content terms are **bold** and are defined at the bottom of the spread where they first appear.

Printed in the United States 5039

Table of Contents

Get Ready for Fun

Swings whoosh through the air. Kids zip down long slides, and swing across monkey bars. There's never a dull moment on a playground. But you need to be safe while having fun. With a few rules, you can stay safe on the playground.

What to Wear

Playground safety starts with your clothes. Avoid clothes that have long strings or ties. Strings could get caught on slides, swings, or other equipment. Always wear shoes when you play, and tie them tightly. Put on sunscreen to avoid getting a sunburn.

Trusted Adults

Staying safe on the playground is easy when you have a **trusted adult** along. Trusted adults are people such as your parents or teachers.

trusted adult—a grown-up you know who is honest and reliable

Adults can help you use equipment the right way. They know if the equipment is right for your age. They can check equipment to make sure it's safe.

Take a Look

When you get to the playground, take a look around. Equipment should be placed over a soft surface. Soft surfaces are **pea gravel**, wood chips, sand, and rubber.

pea gravel—small stones the size of peas

Avoid hard surfaces such as **asphalt**, concrete, dirt, and grass. Make sure there is no broken glass or garbage around equipment.

asphalt—a black tar that is mixed with sand and gravel to make paved surfaces

Equipment Check

Before you play, make sure the equipment is safe. Wet equipment can cause slips or falls. Make sure the equipment isn't broken. Look for any loose parts or open hooks. Tell a trusted adult if you see broken equipment.

Follow the Rules

Playground equipment comes in many shapes and sizes. But each piece is meant to be used a certain way. It isn't safe to stand on swings or jump off tall climbers. Don't climb outside safety railings. Use handrails when climbing up and down equipment.

Safety on Swings

Swings make you feel like you're soaring through air. Avoid crash landings by following a few rules. Always sit down while you swing. Slow down before getting off. You could get hurt if you jump. Do not walk near someone who is swinging. You could get hit if you walk too close.

Safety on Slides

Zipping down slides is always fun. But slides should be used in the right way. Hold onto the ladder when you climb up. Sit down on the slide, and then take a look around. Make sure no one is at the bottom of the slide. Then slide down feet first. Never climb up the front of the slide.

Strangers

Most people at playgrounds are **strangers**. Strangers are people you haven't met. Stay close to your friends and a trusted adult. Never leave with someone you don't know.

stranger—a person you do not know

Hands On: Safety Checklist

Not sure a playground meets the safety rules? A checklist can help you decide whether a playground is safe.

What You Need

paper

pen

What You Do

1. Fold a piece of paper into three sections.
2. Write one of these labels on each section of the paper—clothing, playground area, and equipment.
3. Make a list of safety tips for clothing. Tips can include: *Make sure your shoes are tied.*
4. Write down safety tips for the playground area. Tips can include: *Make sure equipment is placed over a soft surface.*
5. Next write down safety tips for playground equipment. Tips can include: *Make sure equipment is dry.*
6. Use the checklist when you visit playgrounds.

Glossary

asphalt (AS-fawlt)—a black tar that is mixed with sand and gravel to make paved surfaces

concrete (con-CREET)—a mix that gets hard when it dries

pea gravel (PEA GRAV-uhl)—small stones the size of peas

stranger (STRAYN-jur)—a person you do not know

surface (SUR-fiss)—the top layer of something

trusted adult (TRUHS-tud uh-DUHLT)—a grown-up you know who is honest and reliable

Donahue, Jill Urban. *Play It Smart: Playground Safety*. How to Be Safe! Minneapolis: Picture Window Books, 2009.

Knowlton, MaryLee. *Safety at the Playground*. Staying Safe. New York: Crabtree Pub. Co, 2009.

Rissman, Rebecca. *We Can Stay Safe*. Chicago: Heinemann Library, 2010.

FactHound offers a safe, fun way to find Internet sites related to this book. All of the sites on FactHound have been researched by our staff.

Here's all you do:

Visit *www.facthound.com*

Type in this code: 9781429668224

Index